APOSTOLIC LE`

POI

MISERICORDIA
ET MISERA

TO ALL WHO READ THIS APOSTOLIC LETTER
MERCY AND PEACE

*All documents are published thanks to the
generous support of the members of the
Catholic Truth Society*

CATHOLIC TRUTH SOCIETY
PUBLISHERS TO THE HOLY SEE

CONTENTS

*First published 2016 by The Incorporated Catholic Truth Society
40-46 Harleyford Road London SE11 5AY Tel: 020 7640 0042
Fax: 020 7640 0046. Copyright © 2016 Libreria Editrice Vaticana,
Citta del Vaticano.*
Image: The Woman Taken in Adultery. *By Guercino.* © Alamy Stock
Photo / Dulwich Picture Gallery.

ISBN 978 1 78469 168 4

MISERICORDIA ET MISERA

MISERICORDIA ET MISERA is a phrase used by Saint Augustine in recounting the story of Jesus' meeting with the woman taken in adultery (cf. *Jn* 8:1-11). It would be difficult to imagine a more beautiful or apt way of expressing the mystery of God's love when it touches the sinner: "the two of them alone remained: *mercy with misery*".[1] What great mercy and divine justice shine forth in this narrative! Its teaching serves not only to throw light on the conclusion of the Extraordinary Jubilee of Mercy, but also to point out the path that we are called to follow in the future.

THE MERCY OF LOVE

1. This page of the Gospel could easily serve as an icon of what we have celebrated during the Holy Year, a time rich in mercy, which must continue to be celebrated and lived out in our communities. Mercy cannot become a mere parenthesis in the life of the Church; it constitutes her very existence, through which the profound truths of the Gospel are made manifest and tangible. Everything is revealed in mercy; everything is resolved in the merciful love of the Father.

---

[1] *On the Gospel of John*, XXXIII, 5.

A woman and Jesus meet. She is an adulteress and, in the eyes of the Law, liable to be stoned. Jesus, through his preaching and the total gift of himself that would lead him to the Cross, returned the Mosaic Law to its true and original intent. Here what is central is not the law or legal justice, but the love of God, which is capable of looking into the heart of each person and seeing the deepest desire hidden there; God's love must take primacy over all else. This Gospel account, however, is not an encounter of sin and judgement in the abstract, but of a sinner and her Saviour. Jesus looked that woman in the eye and read in her heart a desire to be understood, forgiven and set free. The misery of sin was clothed with the mercy of love. Jesus' only judgement is one filled with mercy and compassion for the condition of this sinner. To those who wished to judge and condemn her to death, Jesus replies with a lengthy silence. His purpose was to let God's voice be heard in the conscience not only of the woman, but also in those of her accusers, who drop their stones and one by one leave the scene (cf. *Jn* 8:9). Jesus then says: "Woman, where are they? Has no one condemned you?… Neither do I condemn you. Go your way and from now on do not sin again" (vv. 10-11). Jesus helps the woman to look to the future with hope and to make

4

a new start in life. Henceforth, if she so desires, she can "walk in charity" (*Ep* 5:2). Once clothed in mercy, even if the inclination to sin remains, it is overcome by the love that makes it possible for her to look ahead and to live her life differently.

FATHER, FORGIVE THEM

2. Jesus had taught this clearly on another occasion, when he had been invited to dine at the home of a Pharisee (cf. *Lk* 7:36-50) and a woman, known by everyone to be a sinner, approached him. She poured perfume over his feet, bathed them with her tears and dried them with her hair (cf. vv. 37-38). To the scandalised reaction of the Pharisee, Jesus replied: "Her sins, which are many, are forgiven, for she loved much; but he who is forgiven little, loves little" (v. 47).

Forgiveness is the most visible sign of the Father's love, which Jesus sought to reveal by his entire life. Every page of the Gospel is marked by this imperative of a love that loves to the point of forgiveness. Even at the last moment of his earthly life, as he was being nailed to the cross, Jesus spoke words of forgiveness: "Father, forgive them; for they know not what they do" (*Lk* 23:34).

Nothing of what a repentant sinner places before God's mercy can be excluded from the embrace of his forgiveness. For this reason, none of us has the right to make forgiveness conditional. Mercy is always a gratuitous act of our heavenly Father, an unconditional and unmerited act of love. Consequently, we cannot risk opposing the full freedom of the love with which God enters into the life of every person.

Mercy is this concrete action of love that, by forgiving, transforms and changes our lives. In this way, the divine mystery of mercy is made manifest. God is merciful (cf. *Ex* 34:6); his mercy lasts for ever (cf. *Ps* 136). From generation to generation, it embraces all those who trust in him and it changes them, by bestowing a share in his very life.

MERCY BRINGS JOY

3. What great joy welled up in the heart of these two women. Forgiveness made them feel free at last and happy as never before. Their tears of shame and pain turned into the smile of a person who knows that he or she is loved. Mercy gives rise to joy, because our hearts are opened to the hope of a new life. The joy of forgiveness is inexpressible, yet it radiates all around us whenever we experience forgiveness. Its source is in the love with which God comes to meet us, breaking through walls of selfishness that surround us, in order to make us in turn instruments of mercy.

How meaningful in this regard are the words of encouragement found in an early Christian text: "Clothe yourselves in joy, which always is agreeable and acceptable to God, and rejoice in it. For all who are joyful do what is good, think what is good, and despise sadness... All who put aside sadness and put on joy will live in God".[2] The experience of mercy brings joy. May we never allow this joy to be robbed from us by our troubles and concerns. May it remain rooted in our hearts and enable us to approach with serenity the events of our daily lives.

In a culture often dominated by technology, sadness and loneliness appear to be on the rise, not least among young people. The future seems prey to an uncertainty that does not make for stability. This often gives rise to depression, sadness and boredom, which can gradually lead to despair. We need witnesses to hope and true joy if we are to dispel the illusions that promise quick and easy happiness through artificial paradises. The profound sense of emptiness felt by so many people can be overcome by the hope we bear in our hearts and by the joy that it gives. We need to acknowledge the joy that rises up in a heart touched by mercy. Let us keep in mind, then, the words of

---

[2] *Shepherd of Hermas*, XLII, 1-4.

the Apostle: "Rejoice in the Lord always" (*Phil* 4:4; cf. *1 Th* 5:16)

THE HOLY YEAR

4. We have celebrated an intense Jubilee Year in which we have received the grace of mercy in abundance. Like a gusting but wholesome wind, the Lord's goodness and mercy have swept through the entire world. Because each of us has experienced at length this loving gaze of God, we cannot remain unaffected, for it changes our lives.

We feel the need above all to thank the Lord and to tell him: "Lord, you have been favourable to your land… You have forgiven the iniquity of your people" (*Ps* 85:1-2). So it is. God has subdued our iniquities and cast all our sins into the depths of the sea (cf. *Mic* 7:19). He no longer remembers them, since he has cast them behind his back (cf. *Is* 38:17). As far as the east is from the west, so far has he removed our transgressions from us (cf. *Ps* 103:12).

In this Holy Year, the Church listened attentively and experienced intensely the presence and closeness of the Father, who with the Holy Spirit has enabled her to see with greater clarity the gift and mandate of Jesus Christ regarding forgiveness. It has truly been like a new visitation of the Lord among us. We have felt his life-giving breath poured out upon the Church and, once again, his words have pointed out our mission: "Receive the Holy Spirit: if you forgive the sins of any, they are forgiven; if you retain the sins of any, they are retained" (*Jn* 20:22-23).

CALLED TO CELEBRATE MERCY

5. Now, at the conclusion of this Jubilee, it is time to look to the future and to understand how best to continue, with joy, fidelity and enthusiasm, experiencing the richness of God's mercy. Our communities can remain alive and active in the work of the new evangelisation in the measure that the "pastoral conversion" to which we are called[3] will be shaped daily by the renewing force of mercy. Let us not limit its action; let us not sadden the Spirit, who constantly points out new paths to take in bringing to everyone the Gospel of salvation.

First, we are called to *celebrate* mercy. What great richness is present in the Church's prayer when she invokes God as the Father of mercies! In the liturgy, mercy is not only repeatedly implored, but is truly received and experienced. From the beginning to the end of the Eucharistic celebration, mercy constantly

---

[3] Cf. Apostolic Exhortation *Evangelii Gaudium*, 27.

appears in the dialogue between the assembly at prayer and the heart of the Father, who rejoices to bestow his merciful love. After first pleading for forgiveness with the invocation "Lord have mercy", we are immediately reassured: "May almighty God have mercy on us, forgive us our sins, and lead us to everlasting life". With this confidence, the community gathers in the presence of the Lord, particularly on the holy day of the resurrection. Many of the "Collect" prayers are meant to remind us of the great gift of mercy. In Lent, for example, we pray: "O God, author of every mercy and of all goodness, who in fasting, prayer and almsgiving have shown us a remedy for sin, look graciously on this confession of our lowliness, that we, who are bowed down by our conscience, may always be lifted up by your mercy".[4] We are immersed in the great Eucharistic Prayer with the Preface that proclaims: "You so loved the world that in your mercy you sent us the Redeemer, to live like us in all things but sin".[5] The Fourth Eucharistic Prayer is a hymn to God's mercy: "For you came in mercy to the aid of all, so that those who seek might find you". "Have mercy on us all"[6] is

---

[4] *Roman Missal*, Opening Prayer for the Third Sunday of Lent.

[5] Ibid., Preface for Sundays in Ordinary Time VII.

[6] Ibid., Eucharistic Prayer II.

the insistent plea made by the priest in the Eucharistic Prayer to implore a share in eternal life. After the *Our Father*, the priest continues by invoking peace and liberation from sin by the "aid of your mercy". And before the sign of peace, exchanged as an expression of fraternity and mutual love in the light of forgiveness received, the priest prays: "Look not upon on our sins but on the faith of your Church".[7] In these words, with humble trust we beseech the gift of unity and peace for Holy Mother Church. The celebration of divine mercy culminates in the Eucharistic Sacrifice, the memorial of Christ's paschal mystery, the source of salvation for every human being, for history and for the whole world. In a word, each moment of the Eucharistic celebration refers to God's mercy.

In the sacramental life, mercy is granted us in abundance. It is not without significance that the Church mentions mercy explicitly in the formulae of the two "sacraments of healing", namely, the sacrament of Penance and Reconciliation and the sacrament of the Anointing of the Sick. In the first, the formula of absolution reads: "God, the Father of mercies, through the death and resurrection of his Son has reconciled the world to himself and sent the Holy Spirit among us

---

[7] Ibid., Communion Rite.

for the forgiveness of sins; through the ministry of the Church may God give you pardon and peace".[8] In the second, the formula of anointing reads: "Through this holy anointing may the Lord in his love and mercy help you with the grace of the Holy Spirit".[9] In the Church's prayer, then, references to mercy, far from being merely exhortative, are highly *performative*, which is to say that as we invoke mercy with faith, it is granted to us, and as we confess it to be vital and real, it transforms us. This is a fundamental element of our faith, and we must keep it constantly in mind. Even before the revelation of sin, there is the revelation of the love by which God created the world and human beings. Love is the first act whereby God reveals himself and turns towards us. So let us open our hearts and trust in God's love for us. His love always precedes us, accompanies us and remains with us, despite our sin.

THE WORD OF GOD

6. In this context, *hearing the word of God* takes on particular significance. Each Sunday, God's word is proclaimed in the Christian community so that the Lord's Day may be illuminated by the paschal

---

[8] *Rite of Penance*, No. 46.

[9] *Sacrament of Anointing and Pastoral Care of the Sick*, No. 76.

mystery.[10] In the Eucharistic celebration, we seem to witness a true dialogue between God and his people. In the biblical readings, we retrace the history of our salvation through the proclamation of God's tireless work of mercy. The Lord continues to speak to us today as to friends; he dwells in our midst,[11] in order to accompany us and show us the path of life. His word gives a voice to our inmost needs and worries, and offers a fruitful response, so that we can concretely experience his closeness to us. Hence the importance of the homily, in which "truth goes hand in hand with beauty and goodness"[12] so that the hearts of believers may thrill before the grandeur of mercy! I strongly encourage that great care be given to preparing the homily and to preaching in general. A priest's preaching will be fruitful to the extent that he himself has experienced the merciful goodness of the Lord. Communicating the certainty that God loves us is not an exercise in rhetoric, but a condition for the credibility of one's priesthood. The personal experience of mercy is the best way to make it a true message of consolation and conversion in the pastoral ministry.

---

[10] Cf. SECOND VATICAN ECUMENICAL COUNCIL, Constitution on the Sacred Liturgy *Sacrosanctum Concilium*, 106.

[11] ID., Dogmatic Constitution *Dei Verbum*, 2.

[12] Apostolic Exhortation *Evangelii Gaudium*, 142.

Both homiletics and catechesis need to be sustained by this pulsing heart of the Christian life.

SACRED SCRIPTURES

7. The *Bible* is the great story of the marvels of God's mercy. Every one of its pages is steeped in the love of the Father who from the moment of creation wished to impress the signs of his love on the universe. Through the words of the prophets and the wisdom writings, the Holy Spirit shaped the history of Israel as a recognition of God's closeness and love, despite the people's infidelity. Jesus' life and preaching decisively marked the history of the Christian community, which has viewed its mission in terms of Christ's command to be a permanent instrument of his mercy and forgiveness (cf. *Jn* 20:23). Through Sacred Scripture, kept alive by the faith of the Church, the Lord continues to speak to his Bride, showing her the path she must take to enable the Gospel of salvation to reach all mankind. I greatly desire that God's word be increasingly celebrated, known and disseminated, so that the mystery of love streaming from this font of mercy may be ever better understood. As the Apostle tells us clearly: "All Scripture is inspired by God and profitable for teaching, for reproof, for correction, and for training in righteousness" (*2 Tm* 3:16).

It would be beneficial if every Christian community, on one Sunday of the liturgical year, could renew its efforts to make the Sacred Scriptures better known and more widely diffused. It would be a Sunday given over entirely to the word of God, so as to appreciate the inexhaustible riches contained in that constant dialogue between the Lord and his people. Creative initiatives can help make this an opportunity for the faithful to become living vessels for the transmission of God's word. Initiatives of this sort would certainly include the practice of *lectio divina*, so that the prayerful reading of the sacred text will help support and strengthen the spiritual life. Such a reading, centred on themes relating to mercy, will enable a personal experience of the great fruitfulness of the biblical text – read in the light of the Church's spiritual tradition – and thus give rise to concrete gestures and works of charity.[13]

SACRAMENT OF FORGIVENESS

8. The celebration of mercy takes place in a very particular way in the *Sacrament of Penance and Reconciliation*. Here we feel the embrace of the Father, who comes forth to meet us and grant us the grace of being once more his sons and daughters. We are sinners

---

[13] Cf. BENEDICT XVI, Post-Synodal Apostolic Exhortation *Verbum Domini*, 86-87.

and we bear the burden of contradiction between what we wish to do and what we do in fact (cf. *Rm* 7:14-21). Yet grace always precedes us and takes on the face of the mercy that effects our reconciliation and pardon. God makes us understand his great love for us precisely when we recognise that we are sinners. Grace is stronger than sin: it overcomes resistance, because love conquers all (cf. *1 Co* 13:7).

In the sacrament of Forgiveness God shows us the way to turn back to him and invites us to experience his closeness anew. This pardon can be obtained by beginning, first of all, to live in charity. The Apostle Peter tells us this when he writes that "love covers a multitude of sins" (*1 P* 4:8). Only God forgives sins, but he asks that we be ready to forgive others even as he has forgiven us: "Forgive us our trespasses, as we forgive those who trespass against us" (*Mt* 6:12). How sad it is when our hearts are closed and unable to forgive! Resentment, anger and revenge gain the upper hand, making our lives miserable and blocking a joyful commitment to mercy.

MISSIONARIES OF MERCY

9. An experience of grace lived out by the Church with great effectiveness in the Jubilee Year has certainly been the service of the *Missionaries of Mercy*. Their

pastoral activity sought to emphasise that God places no roadblocks in the way of those who seek him with a contrite heart, because he goes out to meet everyone like a father. I have received many testimonies of joy from those who encountered the Lord once more in the sacrament of Confession. Let us not miss the opportunity to live our faith also as an experience of reconciliation. Today too, the Apostle urges us: "Be reconciled to God" (*2 Co* 5:20), so that all who believe can discover the power of love which makes us "a new creation" (*2 Co* 5:17).

I thank every Missionary of Mercy for this valuable service aimed at rendering effective the grace of forgiveness. This extraordinary ministry does not end with the closing of the Holy Door. I wish it to continue until further notice as a concrete sign that the grace of the Jubilee remains alive and effective the world over. As a direct expression of my concern and proximity to the Missionaries of Mercy in this period, the Pontifical Council for the Promotion of the New Evangelisation will supervise them and find the most suitable forms for the exercise of this valuable ministry.

HELPING PENITENTS

10. I invite priests once more to prepare carefully for the ministry of confession, which is a true priestly

mission. I thank all of you from the heart for your ministry, and I ask you to be *welcoming* to all, *witnesses* of fatherly love whatever the gravity of the sin involved, *attentive* in helping penitents to reflect on the evil they have done, *clear* in presenting moral principles, *willing* to walk patiently beside the faithful on their penitential journey, *far-sighted* in discerning individual cases and *generous* in dispensing God's forgiveness. Just as Jesus chose to remain silent in order to save the woman caught in adultery from the sentence of death, so every priest in the confessional should be open-hearted, since every penitent is a reminder that he himself is a sinner, but also a minister of mercy.

MINISTRY OF RECONCILIATION

11. I would like us all to meditate upon the words of the Apostle, written towards the end of his life, when he confesses to Timothy that he was the greatest of sinners, "but for this reason I received mercy" (*1 Tm* 1:16). Paul's words, powerful as they are, make us reflect on our lives and see God's mercy at work in changing, converting and reforming our hearts. "I thank him who has given me strength for this, Christ Jesus our Lord, because he judged me faithful

The Woman Taken in Adultery, **by Guercino**

by appointing me to his service, though I formerly blasphemed and persecuted and insulted him. But I received mercy" (*1 Tm* 1:12-13).

Let us recall with renewed pastoral zeal another saying of the Apostle: "God has reconciled us to himself through Christ and has entrusted to us the message of reconciliation" (*2 Co* 5:18). We were the first to be forgiven in view of this ministry, made witnesses at first hand of the universality of God's forgiveness. No law or precept can prevent God from once more embracing the son who returns to him, admitting that he has done wrong but intending to start his life anew. Remaining only at the level of the law is equivalent to thwarting faith and divine mercy. The law has a propaedeutic value (cf. *Ga* 3:24) with charity as its goal (cf. *1 Tm* 1:5). Nonetheless, Christians are called to experience the newness of the Gospel, the "law of the Spirit of life in Christ Jesus" (*Rm* 8:2). Even in the most complex cases, where there is a temptation to apply a justice derived from rules alone, we must believe in the power flowing from divine grace.

We confessors have experienced many conversions that took place before our very eyes. We feel responsible, then, for actions and words that can touch the heart of penitents and enable them to discover the closeness and tenderness of the Father who forgives. Let us not lose such occasions by acting in a way that can contradict the experience of mercy that the penitent seeks. Rather, let us help light up the space of personal conscience with God's infinite love (cf. *1 Jn* 3:20).

The Sacrament of Reconciliation must regain its central place in the Christian life. This requires priests capable of putting their lives at the service of the "ministry of reconciliation" (*2 Co* 5:18), in such a way that, while no sincerely repentant sinner is prevented from drawing near to the love of the Father who awaits his return, everyone is afforded the opportunity of experiencing the liberating power of forgiveness.

A favourable occasion for this could be the *24 Hours for the Lord*, a celebration held in proximity to the Fourth Sunday of Lent. This initiative, already in place in many dioceses, has great pastoral value in encouraging a more fervent experience of the sacrament of Confession.

SPECIAL RECONCILIATION

12. Given this need, lest any obstacle arise between the request for reconciliation and God's forgiveness, I henceforth grant to all priests, in virtue of their ministry,

21

the faculty to absolve those who have committed the sin of procured abortion. The provision I had made in this regard, limited to the duration of the Extraordinary Holy Year,[14] is hereby extended, notwithstanding anything to the contrary. I wish to restate as firmly as I can that abortion is a grave sin, since it puts an end to an innocent life. In the same way, however, I can and must state that there is no sin that God's mercy cannot reach and wipe away when it finds a repentant heart seeking to be reconciled with the Father. May every priest, therefore, be a guide, support and comfort to penitents on this journey of special reconciliation.

For the Jubilee Year I had also granted that those faithful who, for various reasons, attend churches officiated by the priests of the Priestly Fraternity of Saint Pius X, can validly and licitly receive the sacramental absolution of their sins.[15] For the pastoral benefit of these faithful, and trusting in the good will of their priests to strive with God's help for the recovery of full communion in the Catholic Church, I have personally decided to extend this faculty beyond the Jubilee Year, until further provisions are made, lest

---

[14] Cf. *Letter According to Which an Indulgence is Granted to the Faithful on the Occasion of the Extraordinary Jubilee of Mercy*, 1 September 2015.

[15] Cf. ibid.

anyone ever be deprived of the sacramental sign of reconciliation through the Church's pardon.

COMFORT MY PEOPLE

13. Another face of mercy is *consolation*. "Comfort, comfort my people" (*Is* 40:1) is the heartfelt plea that the prophet continues to make today, so that a word of hope may come to all those who experience suffering and pain. Let us never allow ourselves to be robbed of the hope born of faith in the Risen Lord. True, we are often sorely tested, but we must never lose our certainty of the Lord's love for us. His mercy finds expression also in the closeness, affection and support that many of our brothers and sisters can offer us at times of sadness and affliction. The drying of tears is one way to break the vicious circle of solitude in which we often find ourselves trapped.

All of us need consolation because no one is spared suffering, pain and misunderstanding. How much pain can be caused by a spiteful remark born of envy, jealousy or anger! What great suffering is caused by the experience of betrayal, violence and abandonment! How much sorrow in the face of the death of a loved one! And yet God is never far from us at these moments of sadness and trouble. A reassuring word, an embrace that makes us feel

23

understood, a caress that makes us feel love, a prayer that makes us stronger...all these things express God's closeness through the consolation offered by our brothers and sisters.

Sometimes too, *silence* can be helpful, especially when we cannot find words in response to the questions of those who suffer. A lack of words, however, can be made up for by the compassion of a person who stays at our side, who loves us and who holds out a hand. It is not true that silence is an act of surrender; on the contrary, it is a moment of strength and love. Silence also belongs to our language of consolation, because it becomes a concrete way of sharing in the suffering of a brother or sister.

BEAUTY OF THE FAMILY

14. At a time like our own, marked by many crises, including that of the family, it is important to offer a word of comfort and strength to our families. The gift of matrimony is a great calling to which spouses, with the grace of Christ, respond with a love that is generous, faithful and patient. The beauty of the family endures unchanged, despite so many problems and alternative proposals: "The joy of love experienced by families is

also the joy of the Church".[16] The journey of life that leads a man and a woman to meet one other, to love one another and to promise mutual fidelity before God, is often interrupted by suffering, betrayal and loneliness. Joy at the gift of children is accompanied by concern about their growth and education, and their prospects for happiness and fulfilment in life.

The grace of the sacrament of Marriage not only strengthens the family to be a privileged place for practising mercy, but also commits the Christian community and all its pastoral activity to uphold the great positive value of the family. This Jubilee Year cannot overlook the complexity of the current realities of family life. The experience of mercy enables us to regard all human problems from the standpoint of God's love, which never tires of welcoming and accompanying.[17]

We have to remember each of us carries the richness and the burdens of our personal history; this is what makes us different from everyone else. Our life, with its joys and sorrows, is something unique and unrepeatable that takes place under the merciful gaze of God. This demands, especially of priests, a careful, profound and far-sighted spiritual discernment, so that everyone, none

---

[16] Post-Synodal Apostolic Exhortation *Amoris Laetitia*, 1.
[17] Cf. ibid., 291-300.

excluded, can feel accepted by God, participate actively in the life of the community and be part of that People of God which journeys tirelessly towards the fullness of his kingdom of justice, love, forgiveness and mercy.

DEATH MUST BE FACED

15. Here too, we see the particular importance of *the moment of death*. The Church has always experienced this dramatic passage in the light of Christ's resurrection, which opened the way to the certainty of the life to come. We have a great challenge to face, especially in contemporary culture, which often tends to trivialise death to the point of treating it as an illusion or hiding it from sight. Yet death must be faced and prepared for as a painful and inescapable passage, yet one charged with immense meaning, for it is the ultimate act of love towards those we leave behind and towards God whom we go forth to meet. In all religions, the moment of death, like that of birth, is accompanied by a religious presence. As Christians, we celebrate the funeral liturgy as a hope-filled prayer for the soul of the deceased and for the consolation of those who suffer the loss of a loved one.

I am convinced that our faith-filled pastoral activity should lead to a direct experience of how the liturgical signs and our prayers are an expression of the Lord's mercy. It is the Lord himself who offers words of hope, since nothing and no one can ever separate us from his love (cf. *Rm* 8:35). The priest's sharing in this moment is an important form of pastoral care, for it represents the closeness of the Christian community at a moment of weakness, solitude, uncertainty and grief.

ROAD OF MERCY

16. The Jubilee now ends and the Holy Door is closed. But the door of mercy of our heart continues to remain wide open. We have learned that God bends down to us (cf. *Ho* 11:4) so that we may imitate him in bending down to our brothers and sisters. The yearning of so many people to turn back to the house of the Father, who awaits their return, has also been awakened by heartfelt and generous testimonies to God's love. The Holy Door that we have crossed in this Jubilee Year has set us on the *path of charity*, which we are called to travel daily with fidelity and joy. It is the road of mercy, on which we meet so many of our brothers and sisters who reach out for someone to take their hand and become a companion on the way.

The desire for closeness to Christ requires us to draw near to our brothers and sisters, for nothing is more pleasing to the Father than a true sign of mercy. By its very nature, mercy becomes visible and tangible in specific acts. Once mercy has been truly experienced, it is impossible to turn back. It grows constantly and it changes our lives. It is an authentic new creation: it brings about a new heart, capable of loving to the full, and it purifies our eyes to perceive hidden needs. How true are the words of the Church's prayer at the Easter Vigil, after the reading of the creation account: "O God, who wonderfully created human nature and still more wonderfully redeemed it".[18]

Mercy *renews and redeems* because it is an encounter between two hearts: the heart of God who comes to meet us and a human heart. The latter is warmed and healed by the former. Our hearts of stone become hearts of flesh (cf. *Ez* 36:26) capable of love despite our sinfulness. I come to realise that I am truly a "new creation" (*Ga* 6:15): I am loved, therefore I exist; I am forgiven, therefore I am reborn; I have been shown mercy, therefore I have become a vessel of mercy.

THE WEAK AND THE VULNERABLE

17. During the Holy Year, especially on the "*Fridays of Mercy*", I was able to experience in a tangible way the goodness present in our world. Often it remains hidden, since it is daily expressed in discreet and quiet gestures. Even if rarely publicised, many concrete acts

---

[18] *Roman Missal*, Easter Vigil, Prayer after the First Reading.

of goodness and tenderness are shown to the weak and the vulnerable, to those most lonely and abandoned. There are true champions of charity who show constant solidarity with the poor and the unhappy. Let us thank the Lord for these precious gifts that invite us to discover the joy of drawing near to human weakness and suffering. I also think with gratitude of the many volunteers who daily devote their time and efforts to showing God's presence and closeness. Their service is a genuine work of mercy, one that helps many people draw closer to the Church.

WORKS OF MERCY

18. Now is the time to unleash the creativity of mercy, to bring about new undertakings, the fruit of grace. The Church today needs to tell of those "many other signs" that Jesus worked, which "are not written" (*Jn* 20:30), so that they too may be an eloquent expression of the fruitfulness of the love of Christ and the community that draws its life from him. Two thousand years have passed, yet works of mercy continue to make God's goodness visible.

In our own day, whole peoples suffer hunger and thirst, and we are haunted by pictures of children with nothing to eat. Throngs of people continue to migrate from one country to another in search of food, work, shelter and peace. Disease in its various forms is a constant cause of suffering that cries out for assistance, comfort and support. Prisons are often places where confinement is accompanied by serious hardships due to inhumane living conditions. Illiteracy remains widespread, preventing children from developing their potential and exposing them to new forms of slavery. The culture of extreme individualism, especially in the West, has led to a loss of a sense of solidarity with and responsibility for others. Today many people have no experience of God himself, and this represents the greatest poverty and the major obstacle to recognition of the inviolable dignity of human life.

To conclude, the corporal and spiritual works of mercy continue in our own day to be proof of mercy's immense positive influence as a social value. Mercy impels us to roll up our sleeves and set about restoring dignity to millions of people; they are our brothers and sisters who, with us, are called to build a "city which is reliable".[19]

NEW WORKS OF MERCY

19. Many concrete signs of mercy have been performed during this Holy Year. Communities, families and

---

[19] Encyclical Letter *Lumen Fidei*, 50.

individuals have rediscovered the joy of sharing and the beauty of solidarity. But this is not enough. Our world continues to create new forms of spiritual and material poverty that assault human dignity. For this reason, the Church must always be vigilant and ready to identify new works of mercy and to practise them with generosity and enthusiasm.

Let us make every effort, then, to devise specific and responsible ways of practising charity and the works of mercy. Mercy is inclusive and tends to expand in a way that knows no limits. Hence we are called to give new expression to the traditional works of mercy. For mercy overflows, keeps moving forward, bears rich fruit. It is like the leaven that makes the dough rise (cf. *Mt* 13:33), or the mustard seed that grows into a tree (cf. *Lk* 13:19).

We need but think of one corporal work of mercy: "to clothe the naked" (cf. *Mt* 25:36,38,43,44). This brings us back to the beginning, in the Garden of Eden, when Adam and Eve realise that they are naked and, hearing the Lord approaching, feel shame and hide themselves (*Gn* 3:7-8). We know that God punished them, yet he also "made for Adam and for his wife garments of skins, and clothed them" (*Gn* 3:21). He covered their shame and restored their dignity.

Let us think too of Jesus on Golgotha. The Son of God hangs naked on the cross; the soldiers took his tunic and cast lots for it (cf. *Jn* 19:23-24). He has nothing left. The cross is the extreme revelation of Jesus' sharing the lot of those who have lost their dignity for lack of the necessities of life. Just as the Church is called to be the "tunic of Christ"[20] and to clothe her Lord once more, so She is committed to solidarity with the naked of the world, to help them recover the dignity of which they have been stripped. Jesus' words: "I was naked and you clothed me" (*Mt* 25:36), oblige us not to turn our backs on the new forms of poverty and marginalisation that prevent people from living a life of dignity.

Being unemployed or not receiving a sufficient salary; not being able to have a home or a land in which to live; experiencing discrimination on account of one's faith, race or social status: these are just a few of the many examples of situations that attack the dignity of the person. In the face of such attacks, Christian mercy responds above all with vigilance and solidarity. How many situations exist today where we can restore dignity to individuals and make possible a truly humane life! Let us think only about the many children who suffer from forms of violence that rob them of the joy of life. I

---

[20] Cf. CYPRIAN, On the Unity of the Catholic Church, 7.

keep thinking of their sorrowful and bewildered faces. They are pleading for our help to be set free from the slavery of the contemporary world. These children are the young adults of tomorrow. How are we preparing them to live with dignity and responsibility? With what hope can they face their present or their future?

The *social character* of mercy demands that we not simply stand by and do nothing. It requires us to banish indifference and hypocrisy, lest our plans and projects remain a dead letter. May the Holy Spirit help us to contribute actively and selflessly to making justice and a dignified life not simply clichés but a concrete commitment of those who seek to bear witness to the presence of the Kingdom of God.

A CULTURE OF MERCY

20. We are called to promote a *culture of mercy* based on the rediscovery of encounter with others, a culture in which no one looks at another with indifference or turns away from the suffering of our brothers and sisters. *The works of mercy are "handcrafted"*, in the sense that none of them is alike. Our hands can craft them in a thousand different ways, and even though the one God inspires them, and they are all fashioned from the same "material", mercy itself, each one takes on a different form.

The works of mercy affect a person's entire life. For this reason, we can set in motion a real cultural revolution, beginning with simple gestures capable of reaching body and spirit, people's very lives. This is a commitment that the Christian community should take up, in the knowledge that God's word constantly calls us to leave behind the temptation to hide behind indifference and individualism in order to lead a comfortable life free of problems. Jesus tells his disciples: "The poor will always be with you" (*Jn* 12:8). There is no alibi to justify not engaging with the poor when Jesus has identified himself with each of them.

The culture of mercy is shaped in assiduous prayer, in docility to the working of the Holy Spirit, in knowledge of the lives of the saints and in being close to the poor. It urges us not to overlook situations that call for our involvement. The temptation to theorise "about" mercy can be overcome to the extent that our daily life becomes one of participation and sharing. Nor should we ever forget what the Apostle tells us about his meeting with Peter, James and John after his conversion. His words highlight an essential aspect of his own mission and of the Christian life as a whole: "They asked only one thing, that we remember the poor, which was actually what I was eager to do" (*Ga*

2:10). We cannot forget the poor: this is an injunction as relevant today as ever, and one that compels by its evangelical warrant.

THE TIME OF MERCY

21. The Jubilee impresses upon us the words of the Apostle Peter: "Once you had not received mercy, but now you have received mercy" (*1 P* 2:10). Let us not hold on jealously to what we have received, but share it with our brothers and sisters in need, so that they can be sustained by the power of the Father's mercy. May our communities reach out to all who live in their midst, so that God's caress may reach everyone through the witness of believers.

This is the time of mercy. Each day of our journey is marked by God's presence. He guides our steps with the power of the grace that the Spirit pours into our hearts to make them capable of loving. *It is the time of mercy* for each and all, since no one can think that he or she is cut off from God's closeness and the power of his tender love. *It is the time of mercy* because those who are weak and vulnerable, distant and alone, ought to feel the presence of brothers and sisters who can help them in their need. *It is the time of mercy* because the poor should feel that they are regarded with respect and concern by others who have overcome indifference and discovered what is essential in life. *It is the time of mercy* because no sinner can ever tire of asking forgiveness and all can feel the welcoming embrace of the Father.

During the "Jubilee for Socially Excluded People", as the Holy Doors of Mercy were being closed in all the cathedrals and shrines of the world, I had the idea that, as yet another tangible sign of this Extraordinary Holy Year, the entire Church might celebrate, on the Thirty-Third Sunday of Ordinary Time, the *World Day of the Poor.* This would be the worthiest way to prepare for the celebration of the Solemnity of our Lord Jesus Christ, King of the Universe, who identified with the little ones and the poor and who will judge us on our works of mercy (cf. *Mt* 25:31-46). It would be a day to help communities and each of the baptised to reflect on how poverty is at the very heart of the Gospel and that, as long as Lazarus lies at the door of our homes (cf. *Lk* 16:19-21), there can be no justice or social peace. This Day will also represent a genuine form of new evangelisation (cf. *Mt* 11:5) which can renew the face of the Church as She perseveres in her perennial activity of pastoral conversion and witness to mercy.

MOTHER OF MERCY

22. The Holy Mother of God always looks upon us with her eyes of mercy. She is the first to show us the way and to accompany us in our witness of love. As she is often shown in works of art, the Mother of Mercy gathers us all under the protection of her mantle. Let us trust in her maternal assistance and follow her perennial counsel to look to Jesus, the radiant face of God's mercy.

Given in Rome, at Saint Peter's Basilica, on 20 November, the Solemnity of our Lord Jesus Christ, King of the Universe, in the year 2016, the fourth of my Pontificate.

Franciscus

Francis